Personal Services

Careers for Today

Personal Services

Linda Barrett
Galen Guengerich

Franklin Watts

New York • London • Toronto • Sydney

Developed by: Ω Visual Education Corporation
Princeton, NJ

Cover Photograph: © Robert Brenner/PhotoEdit

Photo Credits: p. 6 George Zimbel/Monkmeyer Press; p. 11 Tom
Dunham; p. 12 Arlene Collins/Monkmeyer Press; p. 14 William J.
McCoy/Rainbow; p. 17 Tom Dunham; p. 20 Tom Dunham; p. 23
Robert Brenner/PhotoEdit; p. 26 Rick Kopstein/Monkmeyer Press;
p. 29 David R. Frazier Photolibrary; p. 32 Dan McCoy/Rainbow; p. 35
Tom Dunham; p. 38 Tom Dunham; p. 41 Tom Dunham; p. 44 Tom
Dunham; p. 48 David R. Frazier Photolibrary; p. 50 Tony Freeman/
PhotoEdit; p. 54 Visual Education Archives; p. 56 Tom Dunham; p. 59
Tom Dunham; p. 62 Tony Freeman/PhotoEdit; p. 65 Tom Dunham;
p. 68 Tom Dunham; p. 74 Michael Newman/PhotoEdit; p. 77 Felicia
Martinez/PhotoEdit; p. 80 Tom Dunham.

Library of Congress Cataloging-in-Publication Data

Barrett, Linda.
Personal services / Linda Barrett and Galen Guengerich.
p.   cm. — (Careers for today)
Includes bibliographical references (p.   ) and index.
Summary: Provides vocational guidance for those interested in
service industry careers such as locksmithing, laundry and dry cleaning,
catering, and personal care services. Describes wages and salaries of
these occupations and explains how to write résumés and conduct
interviews.
ISBN 0-531-11103-2
1. Service industries — Vocational guidance — United States.
2. Service industries — United States — Job descriptions.   3. United
States — Occupations. [1. Service industries — Vocational guidance.
2. Vocational guidance.   3. Occupations.]   I. Guengerich, Galen.
II. Title.   III. Series.
HD9981.5.B37   1991
331.7'02—dc20   90-13010 CIP AC

Contents

Introduction

People who provide personal services have been in demand for thousands of years. In ancient times, people hired workers to care for children, make clothing, and cook food. But only a few workers were available for those jobs. Most workers were needed to grow crops, build houses, and defend against enemies.

As time passed, many changes occurred. Better farming methods allowed fewer people to grow more food. So more workers began to make goods. Then machines changed the way things were made. Goods once made by hand could be made by machine. As a result, the goods became cheaper. More people could afford to buy them. The demand for goods increased.

Fifty years ago, most American workers had jobs producing goods. But factories with modern machinery have allowed fewer people to make more goods. As the number of factory jobs dropped, more people entered service careers. Today, most workers produce services. The service industry is the largest part of the American economy. It is also growing the fastest. In 1950, Americans spent 33 percent of their income on services. By 1988, the amount spent on services had increased to 54 percent.

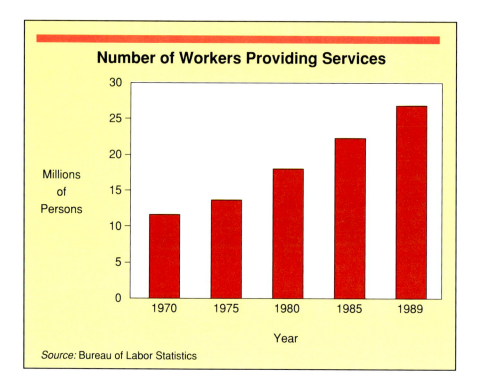

Number of Workers Providing Services

Millions of Persons (y-axis, 0 to 30)

Year (x-axis): 1970, 1975, 1980, 1985, 1989

Source: Bureau of Labor Statistics

As the chart above shows, the number of workers in the service industry has also grown. In fact, the growth of personal services has been especially strong. Why is this so?

In 1930, only about half of all adults held jobs. By 1990, almost two-thirds of the nation's adults were employed. As a result, the demand for personal services has been growing. Many personal service workers come to people's homes. Others work in stores and shops.

This book can help high school students find out about jobs in personal services. The jobs in this field are as varied as the people who fill them. Students can follow their interests and find jobs that are right for them when they graduate.

Personal Services Today

The personal services field includes a wide variety of jobs that may interest graduates: private household worker, building custodian, home caterer, floral designer, furniture upholsterer, tailor or dressmaker, pet care worker, home appliance repairer, locksmith, shoe repairer, pest control worker, laundry and dry-cleaning worker.

The future looks bright for high school graduates interested in jobs in personal services. As the graph below shows, some jobs are growing faster than others are. So it is important to look into a job carefully before making a decision.

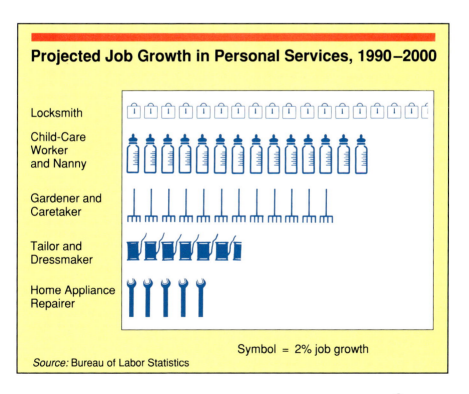

Projected Job Growth in Personal Services, 1990–2000

Locksmith

Child-Care Worker and Nanny

Gardener and Caretaker

Tailor and Dressmaker

Home Appliance Repairer

Symbol = 2% job growth

Source: Bureau of Labor Statistics

Choosing a Career in Personal Services

Personal service workers provide important services to people in many different ways. They may

- Prepare and serve food to guests at weddings and dinner parties
- Get rid of ants, mice, and other pests
- Work for private households driving cars, taking care of gardens, cleaning the household, and providing personal care
- Put in and repair locks and security systems
- Clean buildings and keep them in good repair
- Design floral arrangements
- Repair shoes, boots, handbags, and luggage
- Wash and dry-clean clothing and linens
- Work with dogs, cats, and other small animals
- Fix home appliances
- Put fabric covers on furniture
- Make suits, dresses, shirts, and gowns

People interested in these and other jobs can easily find out more about them. One way to learn is by doing volunteer work. For example, animal shelters often need volunteers to help take care of dogs and cats. Doing this helps a person gain experience. Most employers prefer to hire people with some experience.

People interested in home catering can also volunteer. Meals On Wheels and other groups make meals for elderly people who live at home.

Part-time workers may work at the front desk of a laundry or dry-cleaning shop.

Groups that provide meals for homeless people also need volunteers.

Another good way to learn is by working part-time. High school students can often work in the evening, on weekends, or during vacations. The best places to apply are shops and stores that employ personal service workers. Students may

- Wrap flowers and take orders in a flower shop
- Make keys and sell locks in a hardware store
- Polish shoes and sell supplies in a shoe repair shop
- Work at the front desk of a laundry or dry-cleaning shop
- Care for animals and help customers in a pet shop

Students may also find part-time work in other areas. Some may mow lawns or care for children in a private household. Others may assist a home caterer. These jobs can help students decide which career is right for them. They also may give students a head start in training for a career.

Preparing for a Career in Personal Services

People who want jobs in personal services should begin preparing while in high school. Each job profile in this book lists useful courses students can take.

For many jobs, practical courses such as metal shop, wood shop, carpentry, home economics, and driver's education are helpful. Other useful courses may include art, science, and mechanical drawing. People interested in working for themselves or opening their own businesses should take business courses as well.

Some people may want to take courses beyond high school. Many vocational and technical schools and community colleges offer programs of study to prepare people for personal service careers. These programs may last from several months to two years.

Child-care workers help parents who work outside the home.

Trends in Personal Services

The service area of the economy will continue to grow rapidly. Between 1990 and 2000, the number of service jobs will increase from 32 million to 42.5 million. That means more than 10 million new service workers will be needed.

Many of these workers will work for small businesses. The growth of small service businesses will be very strong in the next ten years. High school students interested in starting a business should look carefully at personal services. Large amounts of money are not usually needed to start personal service businesses. This makes it easier to begin.

One type of service business that is growing very quickly is the personal service agency. These agencies hire workers who can perform many different kinds of personal services. The agencies offer these services to their customers. This system makes it easier for people who need a variety of personal services.

In the future, personal service workers will keep expanding their range of skills. For example, many locksmiths will also be experts in electronic security systems. Shoe repairers will work on luggage and saddles. Changes like these will help personal service businesses continue to grow.

The field of personal services offers many opportunities for a rewarding career. Students should explore a number of options before making a decision. That way, they can be certain the jobs they choose fit their abilities and interests.

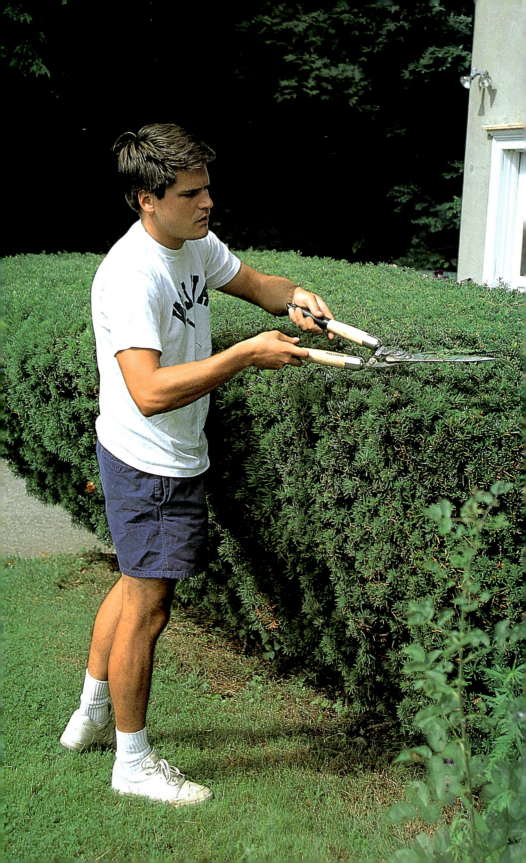

Chapter 1
Private Household Worker

Private household workers work in private homes. They may

- Drive cars
- Maintain lawns and gardens
- Clean and organize the household
- Provide personal care

Some private household workers live in the house. Others live in their own homes and go to work in another household every day.

Education, Training, and Salary

There are no set educational requirements for private household workers. However, many employers prefer to hire people who have a high school education. Workers may find high school courses in home economics, shop, or driver's education helpful.

Private household workers are trained in a number of ways. Many are trained on the job by more experienced workers. Some gain experience working in other places. A driver may have experience driving a taxicab or limousine. A cook may have worked in a restaurant. A companion may have experience as a home health aide. A gardener may have worked for a park service or golf course. Some employers prefer to hire experienced workers. Others are willing to provide on-the-job training.

The pay of private household workers depends on the type of work they do and the demand for household workers in the area. Most are paid by the hour. Their pay ranges from $8,500 to $16,500 a year. Experienced workers can earn more. People who live in the household usually receive free room and board. Most private household workers do not receive benefits.

Job Description

The number of workers in a household varies. Some households employ only one worker. If so, that worker is often a housekeeper. Other households employ ten or more workers. These workers perform a number of different jobs.

Housekeeper   A housekeeper usually organizes the household. In a large household, the housekeeper is the leader of the team of workers. Day workers come to the house to work each day. They clean the rooms, do the laundry, and make the beds. The housekeeper makes sure the day workers do those tasks properly.

If the staff is small, a housekeeper may do these things without help. The housekeeper may also shop for groceries, cook meals, and run errands. Some households hire a cook to plan the menus, order the food, and prepare the meals.

Caretaker and Gardener   These workers maintain the house and the areas around it. Caretakers can make minor repairs both inside and outside the house. They clean windows and gutters, paint fences, and replace light bulbs.

16

A household worker may clean as well as shop and run errands.

They may also paint rooms inside the house and move furniture from one place to another.

In some houses, the caretaker also does the work of a gardener. Other households employ both a caretaker and a gardener. Gardeners mow lawns, trim hedges, plant and weed flower beds and vegetable gardens, and rake leaves. In the winter, the gardener may clear snow and ice from the driveway and sidewalks.

Chauffeur   Chauffeurs drive and maintain the household's vehicles. They drive members of the family to work, school, or social events. Chauffeurs help the people they drive with packages and luggage. Chauffeurs may be asked to run errands as well.

If a vehicle needs to be repaired, the chauffeur makes sure it is done promptly. Keeping vehicles clean is another duty of a chauffeur.

Companions   Companions live with people who do not wish to be alone. They often provide personal care for elderly or handicapped people. If companions are the only household workers, they may also clean the house, cook the meals, and drive the car.

17

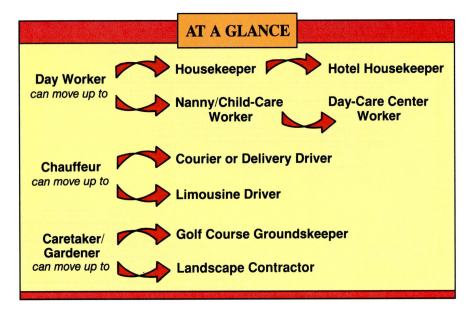

Day Worker
can move up to

Housekeeper

Hotel Housekeeper

Nanny/Child-Care Worker

Day-Care Center Worker

Chauffeur
can move up to

Courier or Delivery Driver

Limousine Driver

Caretaker/ Gardener
can move up to

Golf Course Groundskeeper

Landscape Contractor

Many companions help people who cannot bathe and dress alone. Companions make sure medicines are taken at the proper time. They may also watch television with the people they care for or play games with them. At times companions may read to them. Some companions pay bills, write letters, and take care of other tasks.

Nannies and Child-Care Workers   These workers take care of the infants and children in a household. Nannies often live in the house. Child-care workers usually come to the house every day. Nannies and child-care workers are responsible for the children while their parents are away. The parents may be at work, on a business trip, or away on vacation.

Nannies often receive training for their jobs. They can enroll in training programs that last from a few weeks to two years. Some employers will not hire nannies who have not been trained.

Outlook for Jobs

People interested in becoming private household workers can find out more about these jobs. They can begin by working part-time as a gardener or child-care worker before leaving high school. This will give them an advantage, since many employers look for people with experience and good references.

Working part-time is also a good way for people to find out whether a job suits them. Some people like being part of a private household. Others prefer to work in a company setting.

The demand for private household workers should remain high. In more and more households, both adults have full-time jobs. Many couples hire workers to run the household, look after the children, or care for their elderly parents.

Private household workers can advance by moving to larger households. They may also take on more responsibility. For example, a cook may become a housekeeper, or a gardener may become a caretaker.

For more information on private household workers, write to:

American Home Economic Association
2010 Massachusetts Avenue, NW
Washington, DC 20036

Private Care Association
242 West Valley Avenue
Birmingham, AL 35209
(205) 945–1669

Chapter 2
Building Custodian

Building custodians clean and maintain buildings. To maintain is to keep in working order. They often make minor repairs as well. Some custodians also lock and unlock the buildings. Custodians work in many different types of buildings, including

- Apartment buildings
- Office buildings and business complexes
- Schools, libraries, and other public buildings

The duties of a custodian vary with the type of building. Many custodians work at night when the buildings are empty. Custodians in residential buildings may live in the building. If so, they may be on call at all times.

Education, Training, and Salary

Building custodians do not need to meet any educational requirements. However, many employers prefer to hire people who have a high school education. Students interested in custodial work should take some practical courses. These include courses in working with wood and metal. Knowledge about electricity and plumbing can also be helpful.

Custodians receive on-the-job training. New custodians usually work with experienced custodians. New custodians' first tasks often involve cleaning and routine upkeep. As they gain experience, their duties may include making repairs. Experienced custodians may be responsible for an entire building.

Salaries for building custodians start at about $11,000 a year. Overall, they earn an average of $13,000 a year. Some experienced custodians earn up to $20,000 a year. Benefits usually include paid vacations and holidays, health insurance, and a pension plan. Pension plans provide payments to workers after they retire.

Job Description

The duties of custodians can vary a great deal. In a hospital, custodians may spend most of their time cleaning. In an apartment building, their duties may include making repairs and keeping the building safe. However, the tasks performed by custodians can be divided into four groups.

Cleaning   The main job of custodians is cleaning parts of the building. In an apartment building, custodians usually clean only the public areas. In offices, they clean the entire building.

Custodians keep the floors of the building clean. They vacuum carpeted areas. If the floor is tile or linoleum, they may mop and wax it. Custodians dust desks and other furniture. They clean bathroom fixtures and equipment. As they move through the building, they collect trash and place it in garbage cans or other containers. Many custodians also clean the windows of the building.

Minor Repairs   For some complicated repairs, custodians call a plumber or electrician to

Custodians may work in public buildings as well as apartment buildings or office complexes.

the building. But often custodians can take care of such problems. Custodians change light bulbs that have burned out. They clear clogged drains and fix leaky faucets. Some may repair office chairs or replace broken panes of glass.

General Maintenance   A building is something like a car: It needs regular maintenance in order to work well. Custodians often help with these tasks. They may repaint doors, walls, or even rooms. Custodians usually take care of the furnaces and air-conditioning units. They may need to get rid of insects or other pests. Some custodians also mow lawns, trim hedges, and tend flower beds. In the winter, they clear away ice and snow so people can enter buildings safely.

Administrative Duties   Some custodians help manage the buildings they work in. They may collect rent from the tenants, or residents, of a building. The owner of a building usually sets

23

This morning I came to work an hour early. A new law firm is moving into the third floor today. The firm's office manager wanted to know how the alarm system works. It took only about ten minutes to show her the system. But she wanted to get into the office by 6:30 A.M.

That's part of my job as building custodian. I enjoy being able to help people. And I like getting to know the people who work here. New people enjoy it when I show them around. After seven years on the job, I know this building about as well as I know my own house.

Later in the morning, I had to put new glass in a window on the third floor. One of the movers dropped a bookshelf. It fell against a window and broke the glass. I'm always making little repairs like that. A pane of glass here, a new drawer handle there, a new hinge somewhere else—it takes a lot of work to keep things right.

Most of the time I work during the day. But once in a while I trade with Sam and take the night shift. I like the building when it's empty and quiet. You can mop and wax the floors without anyone walking over them. Of course, sometimes people in the offices work late. I think they like having a custodian here. You see, we keep an eye on things and make people feel safe.

certain rules. The custodians make sure these rules are followed. Custodians often lock and unlock a building's main doors at the proper times.

Custodians know a lot about their buildings and how they work. As a result, people may come to them with questions. They may ask where to put the trash or what hours the front door is unlocked. Custodians help the building run smoothly by answering these questions.

Outlook for Jobs

High school students interested in custodial work can often begin by working part-time. Many janitorial services hire people to clean buildings in the evening or on weekends.

Custodians can advance as they gain experience. Some move to larger buildings. There they supervise the work of other custodians. A few start custodial businesses of their own. The job outlook is best for custodians who can do repair work.

The demand for custodians continues to grow. More and more office and apartment buildings are being built. Each new building will need one or more custodians. Many custodians now work for custodial companies. These companies often provide custodial services for a number of buildings.

For more information on building custodians, write to:

Service Employees International Union
1313 L Street, NW
Washington, DC 20005
(202) 898–3200

Chapter 3
Home Caterer

Home caterers prepare food and serve it to groups of people. These groups include people attending wedding receptions, dinner parties, business lunches, and other functions. Home caterers usually cook the food at home and then take it to the place where the party or dinner is held. They may also take along flowers and ornaments to decorate the room and tables.

Education, Training, and Salary

Above all, a home caterer must be a good cook. But a caterer should also be organized, work well under pressure, and have good business skills.

Home caterers are usually self-employed. For this reason, they do not need to meet any education requirements. However, they do need to learn certain basic skills. One good way to learn these skills is to take home economics courses in high school.

Some people train for home catering by taking courses at trade schools and community colleges. These courses increase a person's chances of becoming a successful home caterer. Students learn how to plan menus, figure costs, and cook a variety of foods. They may also study health rules, local laws, and small-business management. In many areas, people can attend seminars, or special meetings, on management.

Many home caterers learn their skills by working for other people. Some work as cooks in restaurants. Others help prepare and serve dinners in hotels. Working for a catering company is another good way to gain experience.

Since home caterers are self-employed, their income varies greatly. Earnings from catering a large wedding reception will be higher than those from catering a small luncheon. Also, some caterers serve many events every month, while others serve only one or two. Beginning home caterers may earn around $13,000 a year. However, experienced home caterers can earn $25,000 a year or more. Home caterers must provide their own benefits.

Job Description

The first task of a home caterer is to find clients, or customers. Many caterers advertise their services in local newspapers. Some get in touch with organizations that are likely to give dinners and hold other special events.

Clients often want the caterer to give an estimate of the cost of providing the food. An estimate is a guess based on experience. In order to give an estimate, the caterer needs to know

- What type of function the client is planning
- How many people will attend
- The exact menu to be served

Once the client and the caterer agree on a menu and price, the next stage of the work begins. Caterers make a list of all the food and supplies they will need. They buy these items at a

A caterer needs a van to transport food and supplies.

grocery store or have them delivered by a whole-sale food company. Wholesale food companies deal in very large amounts of food. Sometimes caterers provide the dishes, silverware, glasses, and table linens. If they do not own enough of those things, they can arrange to rent them. Most caterers also supply flowers and other decorations. If the event is held outside, the client may want the caterer to provide a tent or canopy. A canopy has a top supported by poles but has no sides.

Whenever possible, home caterers prepare the food ahead of time. Most caterers hire assistants to help them prepare and serve the food. On the day of the event, all the food and supplies must be taken to the proper place. The caterers and their assistants set the tables and arrange the decorations. They finish cooking the food, if necessary, and place it on serving dishes.

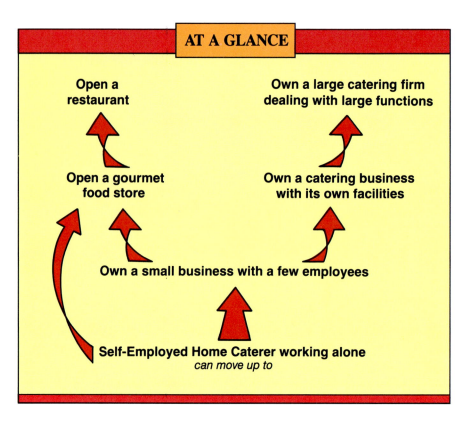

AT A GLANCE

Open a
restaurant

Own a large catering firm
dealing with large functions

Open a gourmet
food store

Own a catering business
with its own facilities

Own a small business with a few employees

Self-Employed Home Caterer working alone
can move up to

If the event is a dinner, the caterers may serve people seated at tables. At a buffet, people serve themselves from large platters of food. At buffets, caterers refill the platters of food when necessary. After the meal, the caterers and their staff may clear away and wash the dishes.

Outlook for Jobs

Home catering is a good career choice for people who enjoy cooking and want their own business. It is not a difficult career to enter. However, people who cook for large groups need a well-equipped kitchen. They also need a number of assistants to help them.

Many people gain experience by working for a caterer or a restaurant. Then they begin working part-time in their own catering business. After the business gets going, they can leave their other jobs. The future is bright for people who want to become home caterers. Wedding receptions and family reunions are as popular as ever. Also, many people today work long hours and do not have time to plan dinner parties. Some call on caterers to plan and prepare these meals.

Businesses are calling on caterers for more and more services. They may want to entertain clients, give employee parties, or hold lunch meetings at their offices.

Home caterers can begin small and develop a large business over time. However, they must be willing to work very hard. Caterers often need to work during the evening and on weekends. Like other small-business owners, they may have little time off. When they are not buying or cooking food, they are selling their services to new customers. The challenges of being a home caterer are great. But the rewards can be great as well.

For more information on home caterers, write to:

Mobile Industrial Caterers Association
7300 Artesia Boulevard
Buena Park, CA 90621

National Association for the Specialty Food Trade
14229 Bessemer Street
Van Nuys, CA 91401
(818) 997–0569

Chapter 4
Floral Designer

Floral designers work in flower shops. They design floral arrangements for special events. These events include

- Weddings
- Birthday and anniversary parties
- Funerals
- Dinner dances and banquets
- Holidays and other special occasions

Floral designers use real and artificial flowers, grasses, and leaves to make the arrangements. Many designers own their own flower shops. They may also provide flower arrangements for catering companies, restaurants, decorators, hotels, and offices.

Education, Training, and Salary

People who want to be floral designers need a high school education. They should take as many art courses as they can. People interested in opening their own shops should take business courses as well.

Floral designers receive on-the-job training. They may also take floral design courses offered by vocational schools or community colleges. It takes about two years to become a fully trained floral designer. Experienced designers help new designers. As they gain skill, new designers are able to do more work on their own. The first stage of training involves making arrangements designed by someone else. In time, designers learn to create their own arrangements.

Floral designers in training earn between $12,000 and $15,000 a year. Experienced designers can earn $20,000 or more a year. Designers who own their shops can earn even more. Benefits usually include paid vacations and holidays. Some employers also provide health insurance and a pension plan. Self-employed workers must provide their own benefits.

Job Description

When people need flowers, they contact a flower shop. Sometimes people go into the shop personally. At other times they call the shop with an order. Many shops also receive orders from people in distant places through a computer network.

The customers usually say what occasion the flowers are for. Some customers tell the designer exactly how they want the flowers to look. Others leave the design up to the floral designer. However, many customers want to discuss the flowers with the designer.

The designers must keep in mind the type of flowers available and the current trends in floral design. They must also consider the event. A wedding bouquet is not the same as a Christmas wreath. Often designers will show their customers photos of flower arrangements. They discuss the number of arrangements the customers will need and what colors would be best. Designers may suggest several designs, each using differ-

34

A floral designer artfully arranges a bouquet.

ent flowers. The customers may also want an estimate of how much the flowers will cost.

Once these decisions are made, the designers begin their work. They use their knowledge of flowers and their design skills to create the arrangement. Designers select flowers that will look their best during the event. They arrange the flowers in special baskets and pots. Then they use floral tape or plastic foam holders to hold the flowers in position.

The designers prepare the finished flowers for delivery. They may cover the flowers with wrapping to protect them. Sometimes they fill out a card telling who the flowers are from. The flowers are then delivered to the correct home, office, or other place.

Some floral designers have other duties as well. They may answer questions from customers

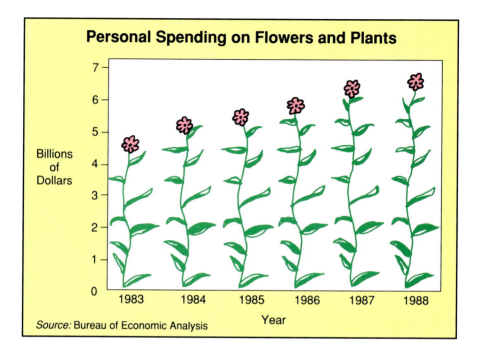

Personal Spending on Flowers and Plants

Billions of Dollars

Source: Bureau of Economic Analysis

Year

in the flower shop. Many customers buy bouquets of cut flowers. The designers help customers select a bouquet. Then the designers wrap the flowers and take the payment.

Floral designers who own their own shops have business matters to take care of. They often hire assistants to help them run the shop. They place advertisements in newspapers and magazines or on radio or television. Some owners keep the financial records themselves. Others hire a bookkeeper to pay bills, record income, and pay taxes.

Some floral designers teach flower-arranging classes. These classes may be offered by a local community college or adult-education program. Other designers give demonstrations at arts and crafts shows.

36

Outlook for Jobs

People interested in floral design can often work part-time while in high school. Many flower shops hire part-time workers to tend the shop and deliver flowers.

Experienced floral designers may become managers of large flower shops. They direct flower design and teach new designers. Some designers choose to open their own shops. A few designers are self-employed. These designers often work out of their homes. With more training, floral designers can become ornamental horticultural technicians. These workers specialize in growing shrubs, hedges, and trees as well as flowers.

The number of floral designers is expected to increase through the year 2000. People enjoy beautiful flower arrangements. As the chart on the facing page shows, each year they spend more money on flowers. And artistic designers are needed to create these arrangements.

For more information on floral designers, write to:

American Institute of Floral Designers
720 Light Street
Baltimore, MD 21230
(301) 752–3318

Society of American Florists
1601 Duke Street
Alexandria, VA 22314
(703) 836–8700

Chapter 5
Furniture Upholsterer and Tailor or Dressmaker

Furniture upholsterers, tailors, and dressmakers work with fabric. Furniture upholsterers remove worn fabric from chairs and couches. They repair the frames and springs and then put on new covers. Tailors and dressmakers use fabric to make clothes for people. Tailors make suits and coats. Dressmakers make dresses, shirts, and wedding gowns.

Furniture Upholsterers

Education, Training, and Salary Most employers prefer to hire people who have a high school education. Upholsterers find courses in woodworking, drafting, and art helpful. New workers can train on the job. It takes about three years to become an upholsterer. Some workers enter an apprentice program for three to four years. They have classroom training and work with experienced upholsterers. Custom upholsterers make furniture to order. They train in a furniture factory or custom upholstery business. Sometimes they work with leather or vinyl.

Upholsterers earn between $12,500 and $14,500 a year to start. Experienced upholsterers can earn $30,000 or more a year. The pay of self-employed upholsterers can vary greatly over time. Benefits usually include paid vacations and holidays. Some employers also provide health insurance and a pension plan. Self-employed workers must provide their own benefits.

Job Description   Furniture upholsterers help customers choose new fabrics for their couches and chairs. They estimate the amount of fabric needed and the total cost of the project. When the customer decides to go ahead, the work begins.

An upholsterer uses hand tools to remove the old fabric and padding. He or she checks the frame and glues any loose joints. The webbing that holds the springs in place may need to be replaced. Broken springs are also replaced. Then the springs are covered with padding.

Using the old fabric as a pattern, the upholsterer cuts new fabric to cover the frame. He or she may sew pieces of the fabric together on a heavy-duty sewing machine. Then the fabric is fastened to the frame with staples and tacks. The final sewing and finishing are done by hand. The upholsterer also makes new covers for cushions.

Outlook for Jobs   People who are interested in becoming upholsterers may gain some experience by working part-time. Some find jobs in furniture factories. Others pick up and deliver furniture for upholsterers.

Upholsterers can advance as they gain experience. They may become supervisors or managers of large shops. Some experienced upholsterers open their own shops.

The number of jobs for furniture upholsterers will not grow quickly. Upholstered furniture costs

40

An upholsterer can make old furniture look new.

less than it once did. Many people replace their furniture rather than having it upholstered again. However, other people do not want to give up their furniture. Upholsterers who can restore valuable furniture are in the greatest demand.

Tailors and Dressmakers

Education, Training, and Salary   Tailors and dressmakers do not need to meet any educational requirements. However, many employers prefer to hire people who have a high school education. While in school, students should take courses in sewing, art, and design.

Some trade schools and junior colleges offer courses in tailoring, dressmaking, and clothing design. Tailors and dressmakers also receive on-the-job training.

Tailors and dressmakers earn an average of $15,500 a year. Experienced workers can earn $18,000 or more a year. Tailors and dressmakers who work in major cities or make expensive clothes can earn much more. Benefits usually include paid vacations and holidays. Some employers also provide health insurance and a pension plan. Self-employed workers must provide their own benefits.

Job Description   Tailors make clothes for men. Dressmakers make clothes for women. Tailors and dressmakers find out what clothing their customers want. They show the customers different fabric samples. Tailors and dressmakers may have different styles of suits, shirts, or dresses on hand for customers to look at. The customers make their decisions. The tailors and dressmakers measure the customers and record the orders.

The tailor or dressmaker may use a standard pattern or make a new one. The pattern is used to cut out the fabric. Then the tailor or dressmaker bastes, or sews lightly, the pieces together. At this point, the garment is fitted on the customer. If necessary, changes are made in the garment.

When the fit is right, the tailor or dressmaker sews the garment together. Some of the sewing is done by machine. The finishing stitching is done by hand. The tailor or dressmaker may also sew other stiff fabric or padding into the garment. These materials help it hold its shape. The tailor or dressmaker attaches buttons, makes buttonholes, and sews in zippers and fasteners. When the garment is finished, it is carefully pressed.

Many tailors and dressmakers also alter (make changes in) and repair clothing for customers. Many are self-employed and work from their homes. Others work in small shops.

42

Outlook for Jobs Tailors and dressmakers can develop their skills in many ways. They may

- Make clothing for themselves and their friends
- Work in a garment factory
- Alter clothing for customers in a department store or dry-cleaning business
- Perform simple sewing and pressing tasks in a tailor or dressmaking shop

As they gain experience, tailors and dressmakers can advance. They work on more complex garments. Some supervise other workers or start their own businesses.

The demand for tailors and dressmakers will continue to increase for the next ten years. Even more workers will be needed to replace people who retire or take other jobs.

For more information on furniture upholsterers, tailors, and dressmakers, write to:

Custom Tailors and Designers Association of America
17 East Forty-fifth Street
New York, NY 10017
(212) 661–1960

National Association of Professional Upholsterers
P.O. Box 2754
200 South Main
High Point, NC 27261
(919) 889–0113

KENNEL HOURS
9AM - 12 NOON
5 - 6:30 PM

NO EXCEPTIONS

Chapter 6
Pet Care Worker

Pet care workers work with small animals, such as dogs, cats, and birds. Some pet care workers breed animals or sell them to people who want pets. Others train the animals, wash or brush their hair, or take care of them while their owners are away. Still others assist with veterinary care. Veterinarians are animal doctors. Pet care workers do their jobs in many places, including

- Pet shops
- Boarding kennels
- Veterinary offices and animal hospitals
- Animal shelters

Education, Training, and Salary

Most pet care workers do not need to meet any educational requirements. However, some employers prefer to hire people who have a high school education. People who want to open their own shops should complete high school. They should take as many business courses as they can. All pet care workers benefit from courses in biology and other sciences.

More than anything else, pet care workers must be able to work well with animals. Many have had pets since they were very young. Some have worked as volunteers in animal shelters. Others have worked part-time in pet shops or boarding kennels. This background helps them learn to work with animals.

Most pet care workers are trained on the job. They help experienced workers do their jobs. Pet care groups offer special courses for some jobs, such as dog groomer and animal trainer.

The pay of pet care workers varies widely. Many pet shop workers and kennel attendants begin at about $8,500 a year. Experienced dog groomers can earn up to $18,000 a year. People who own their businesses may earn $30,000 a year or even more, depending on the size of the business. Benefits usually include paid vacations and holidays. Some employers also provide health insurance and a pension plan. Self-employed workers must provide their own benefits.

Job Description

Pet care workers do many tasks. Each worker cares for pets in a certain way. The different tasks can be grouped into five main jobs.

Animal Breeder Animal breeders raise dogs, cats, rabbits, birds, fish, and other animals for pets. They take care of baby animals from the time the animals are born. Most specialize in one breed, such as poodles or miniature rabbits. They raise the animals until they are old enough to sell. Then they sell them to pet shops or directly to customers.

Animal Trainer Animal trainers teach animals to behave in certain ways. Most trainers work with dogs. They can train dogs to be good house pets. Some trainers teach dogs to act as

Yesterday was a busy day at the kennel. In fact, we have been full for most of the past month. Summer is always a busy time. That's when a lot of people take their vacations.

We can board about forty dogs and twenty-five cats at one time. I work mostly with the dogs. They have to be fed twice a day. And we make sure each one gets enough exercise. We have a fenced-in yard behind the kennel. The dogs can run there. Sometimes I play fetch with them.

Yesterday morning, Mr. Miles brought his black Labrador retriever in. His name is Othello. He will stay until the end of the week, when Mr. Miles gets back from his trip. I like making friends with the dogs and cats, especially when I know they will be back again. I'm sure they recognize me.

guides for blind people. Others may train guard dogs or police dogs. Some of these workers have received special training.

Pet Shop Owner and Worker   Many people buy their pets from local pet shops. The pet shop owners and workers buy animals from breeders. They take care of these pets while they are living in the shop. When customers come in, the owners and workers help them choose a pet. They explain how to care for the pet. Pet shops also sell pet food and other supplies.

Animal Groomer   Animal groomers work in pet shops and in special grooming shops. Some groomers have mobile vans they drive to customers' homes. Most groomers care for dogs. They clean, clip, and brush their coats. They may bathe the animals and treat them for fleas and ticks.

47

An animal groomer keeps pets' coats healthy with frequent shampoos and brushings.

Trimming the animals' hair is another job groomers do. Some groomers prepare animals for dog and cat shows.

Kennel Owner and Attendant   Many people take their pets to kennels when they go away. Kennel owners and attendants take care of their pets. They mainly care for dogs and cats. They feed the animals and keep the places where the animals live clean. Each day, they exercise the dogs. They also watch the animals carefully for signs of sickness. If necessary, they treat the animals or take them to a veterinarian. Kennel attendants work in animal shelters, boarding kennels, and animal hospitals.

Outlook for Jobs

Pet care workers can advance as they gain experience. They can take on extra duties. Some become supervisors or managers in large pet shops, kennels, animal hospitals, or training centers. Workers can also specialize in breeding or training animals. Some workers choose to open their own businesses.

The future for pet care workers is promising. However, a number of people often apply for each job. People with some experience have an advantage.

For more information on pet care workers, write to:

American Animal Hospital Association
1746 Cole Boulevard
Building 21, Suite 150
Golden, CO 80401
(303) 279–2500

National Dog Groomers Association of America
P.O. Box 101
Clark, PA 16113
(412) 962–2711

Chapter 7
Home Appliance Repairer

Home appliances have made many household tasks easier. Imagine what life would be like without modern appliances such as

- Washers, dryers, and irons
- Refrigerators, freezers, and microwaves
- Ranges, toaster ovens, and coffee makers
- Vacuum cleaners and power tools

The number of appliances in each home has increased greatly. As a result, people are needed to install (put in) and repair appliances. Home appliance repairers provide this service.

Education, Training, and Salary

Most employers require their home appliance repairers to have a high school education. They may also look for courses in industrial arts, math, electronics, and physics. These courses help workers learn the job more easily. Some high schools offer courses in appliance repair.

Many employers hire people who have attended vocational or technical school. The people they hire have taken courses in appliance repair, electricity, and electronics. Many appliances now contain electronic parts. Repairers need to know how to repair or replace these parts.

Most employers provide on-the-job training. Some appliance manufacturers offer short training courses as well. The training for the job may include some classroom or home study.

The pay for home appliance repairers varies with the employer and the type of appliance. Repairers start at about $8,500 a year. Experienced appliance repairers can earn $24,000 or more a year. Benefits usually include paid vacations and holidays. Some employers also provide health insurance and a pension plan. Self-employed workers must provide their own benefits.

Job Description

What do people do when the washer will not spin? Where do they turn when the food in the freezer is melting? Who can deal with a vacuum cleaner that does not work? A home appliance repairer is the answer to all these problems.

People can take small appliances to a repair shop to have them fixed. Repairers usually come to people's homes to fix refrigerators and other large appliances. Some repairers work on all types of appliances. Others specialize in one type.

The repairer listens to the customer explain what is wrong. The repairer may ask questions to help identify the problem. The customer may want an estimate of the cost of the repair. The repairer may be able to give a price on the spot. Or he or she may need to check the appliance further.

Often repairers will refer to manuals and diagrams. These give important information about how a certain appliance is made and works. Repairers check electric cords and connections to

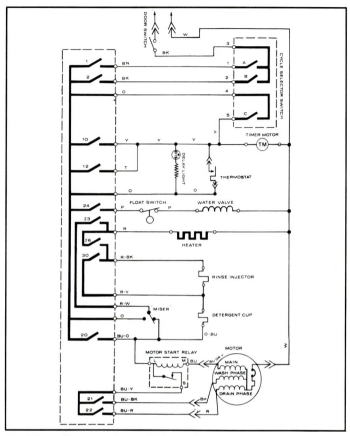

A wiring diagram for a dishwasher

make sure they are not causing the problem. Then they use hand tools to take the appliances apart. As they do this, they check each part of the machine to see if it is faulty. They can use special meters to check the electrical system.

A toaster may need a new heating element. A washer may need a new belt or a bearing. Refrigerators and freezers often need to have coolant added to their cooling systems. The electronic circuit board that controls an appliance may have

A home appliance repairer working on a vacuum cleaner

to be replaced. Repairers may have these items in their shops or vehicles. Some parts may be ordered from a parts dealer.

The repairers remove the faulty part and install a new one. They may use special tools provided by the manufacturer. Then they put the appliance back together. They operate it to make sure it works properly.

Some home appliance repairers also install appliances such as washers, dryers, and dishwashers. They connect the appliances to electric and gas lines. Washers and dishwashers must be hooked up to water lines. Dryers have vent pipes that must be installed. Repairers also test the machines. They do all their work according to certain safety rules. And they explain to the customers how to operate the appliances safely.

Outlook for Jobs

Home appliance repairers in large service centers and shops can advance as they gain experience. Some experienced repairers help train new workers. Others become service supervisors or managers. With more training, repairers may become managers of departments that sell parts. A few take jobs selling new appliances or appliance parts.

In recent years, appliances have become more reliable. As a result, the total number of home appliance repair jobs will not increase. However, new repairers will be needed to replace those who retire or take other jobs. Repairers with training in electronics will be in greatest demand.

For more information on home appliance repairers, write to:

Association of Home Appliance Manufacturers
20 North Wacker Drive
Chicago, IL 60606
(312) 984–5800

Gas Appliance Manufacturers Association
1901 North Moore Street
Arlington, VA 22209

National Appliance Service Association
406 West Thirty-fourth Street
Kansas City, MO 64111
(816) 753–0210

Chapter 8
Locksmith

Locksmiths work with locks and other security devices. They install new locks and repair broken ones. They open locks for people who have lost their keys. Some locksmiths give advice about alarm systems to their customers.

Many locksmiths own their own businesses. Locksmiths also work for

- Locksmith shops and hardware stores
- Large department stores
- Lock and safe manufacturers
- Large factories or warehouses

Education, Training, and Salary

Most employers prefer to hire people who have a high school education. They may also look for people who have taken certain courses. These courses often include mathematics, mechanical drawing, and machine shop.

Locksmiths are trained on the job. It takes several years to learn all about the job. Some new locksmiths take courses as well. They can attend a vocational or technical school. Or they may take courses for locksmiths by mail.

Some new locksmiths become apprentices. They work and study under an experienced locksmith. This type of training usually lasts four years.

New locksmiths can earn about $16,500 a year. Experienced workers earn between $20,000 and $30,000 a year. Locksmiths who work in a large shop or own their own business may earn even more. Benefits usually include paid vacations and holidays. Some employers also provide health insurance and a pension plan. Self-employed workers must provide their own benefits.

Job Description

Almost everyone loses a key now and then. Other times a key may break off inside the lock. Some people keep spare keys to their homes, offices, or cars. But if their only key is lost, or if the lock is broken or jammed, they need help. Often they call locksmiths.

A locksmith usually goes to a location in a truck or van. This vehicle contains the special tools and equipment the locksmith needs. Many locksmiths have well-equipped shops in their vans.

Sometimes the locksmith can make a replacement key for the lock. He or she uses information about the lock and a key-cutting machine to cut a new key. Or the locksmith may open the lock using special tools called picklocks. However, some locks cannot be opened in this way. If not, or if the key has broken off in the lock, a locksmith may drill out the lock. The entire lock will then have to be replaced.

Locksmiths work on combination locks and safes as well. They can open these locks by listening for certain parts inside the lock to fall into place. Some customers want the combinations on their locks changed. Locksmiths can do this by

Locksmiths work on a variety of locks.

replacing the inside of the lock. Or they may file down parts of the lock.

When a lock has to be repaired, the locksmith takes it apart. The locksmith cleans the lock and replaces worn parts. Sometimes the locksmith makes new parts, using hand tools and machines. A locksmith also may work on padlocks, suitcase locks, car locks, bicycle locks, and other types of locks.

Some locksmiths advise people on the security of their homes and businesses. They look at the location of doors, windows, and other openings. They suggest how to lock each opening securely. If the building is large, they may suggest a central locking system. They install these systems and keep a record of the keys each system uses. Using

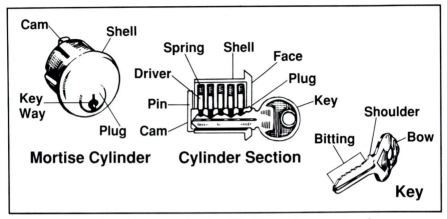

The locksmith learns to identify the various parts of a lock and its key.

this record, locksmiths can make replacement keys quickly.

Today many locksmiths install and repair electronic security systems. These systems link door and window locks to alarm systems. They are often controlled by small computers. Locksmiths can design a security system to meet the needs of the customer.

Locksmiths who own their own businesses have other duties as well. They advertise their services to the public. They meet with customers, take orders, and buy supplies. As the business grows, a locksmith may hire other people to help do the work. Like other business owners, they must also keep records and pay bills.

Outlook for Jobs

High school students interested in becoming locksmiths may be able to begin learning while still in school. Some locksmith shops hire part-time workers to take customer orders. The duties of hardware store employees may include cutting keys and selling locks.

Locksmiths can advance as they gain experience. Some become supervisors or managers in large shops. Others start their own businesses. The Associated Locksmiths of America helps locksmiths keep up to date. Locksmiths can take courses on new types of locks, new tools and equipment, and new methods of opening and repairing locks.

The outlook for locksmiths continues to improve. People are more concerned than ever before about the security of their homes and businesses. The demand for locksmiths will grow faster than the demand for most other jobs will. The need will be greatest for locksmiths who install and repair electronic locking and alarm systems.

For more information on locksmiths, write to:

Associated Locksmiths of America
3003 Live Oak Drive
Dallas, TX 75204
(214) 827–1701

Locksmith Security Association
32630 Concord Drive
Madison Heights, MI 48071

National Locksmith Suppliers Association
1800 Arch Street
Philadelphia, PA 19103

Chapter 9
Shoe Repairer

Shoe repairers repair and refinish items made of leather and other materials. These include

- Shoes and boots
- Luggage and handbags
- Saddles and bridles for horses
- Leather clothing and belts
- Tents, sports equipment, and sports bags

Shoe repairers are skilled at cutting and sewing heavy materials. They work in shoe repair shops, department stores, as well as some dry-cleaning stores. About half of all shoe repairers own their own businesses.

Education, Training, and Salary

Shoe repairers do not need to meet any educational requirements. However, most employers prefer to hire people who have a high school education. Some look for people who have taken high school courses in industrial arts. Students interested in owning or managing a shop should take business courses.

Most shoe repairers train on the job. They begin by doing simple tasks, such as polishing shoes and taking customer orders. They learn more complex skills by helping experienced repairers. Some new shoe repairers become apprentices. It takes about two years for them to become fully trained repairers.

Shoe repairers can also train at a vocational or trade school. They take classes for six months to two years. Then they work in a repair shop for two years to gain experience.

The pay for shoe repairers ranges from $13,000 to $18,000 a year. People who own their own businesses may earn more. The earnings of shoe repairers also vary with the size of the shops they work in. Benefits usually include paid vacations and holidays. Some employers also provide health insurance and a pension plan. Self-employed workers must provide their own benefits.

Job Description

People buy leather shoes because they look nice, feel good, and last a long time. But after a while, the heels and soles become worn. They need to be replaced. Shoe repairers spend most of their time putting new soles and heels on leather shoes.

The repairer places the shoes upside down on stands called lasts. Using special tools, he or she removes the heels. If the soles are worn thin, they are removed as well. The repairer then uses an electric sanding wheel to roughen the bottom edge of the shoe. This makes it easier to attach the new sole properly.

The repairer cuts a new sole from a piece of leather or some other strong material. At this point, the sole is cut slightly too large. The new sole and heel are fastened to the shoe. The repairer may glue and nail them together. Or he or she may sew them by hand or by machine. Next, the repairer uses a knife to trim the sole to fit the shoe exactly. Then the shoe is taken off the last.

64

With a special wheel, the edges of the heel and sole are smoothed and polished.

Shoe repairers repair many other items as well. They may

- Stitch shoe and boot seams that have ripped. Repairers sew these seams by hand or by machine
- Cut new holes in leather belts or make the belts shorter
- Replace zippers in tents and leather clothing
- Sew new straps or buckles onto leather luggage and handbags
- Repair baseball gloves and sports bags
- Stretch leather shoes that are too small to fit the customer comfortably
- Dye shoes, leather jackets, and handbags
- Adjust the fit of orthopedic shoes. These are shoes designed to help people who have problems with their feet

A shoe repairer also works on purses, luggage, and other leather items.

Americans buy over 1 billion pairs of shoes each year. The average American bought four new pairs of shoes last year. Each had many styles to choose from.

You can buy dress shoes with high heels, low heels, or no heels at all. Some come with open toes; others have tassels on top. You can slip them on or lace them up.

Are you a sports fan? High-top basketball shoes may help your game. Or you may choose tennis shoes, volleyball shoes, or special shoes for football, track, cycling, field hockey, or wrestling.

You may need a pair of work shoes as well. Steel-toed construction boots and white medical shoes are only two of the many options.

With so many shoes to choose from, it's hard to believe the average American buys only four pairs a year.

Shoe repairers also help run the shops they work in. They give customers an estimate of the cost of the repairs. When customers bring in shoes, repairers fill out work orders. They also take payments and sell shoe polish, leather cleaner, and other supplies.

The owners or managers of shops have extra duties. They order material for soles and heels as well as other leather supplies. They also pay the employees and keep records.

Outlook for Jobs

People interested in shoe repair can often begin while in high school. Many shops hire part-time workers to help customers. These workers may also learn to do simple repair jobs. Those with some vocational training will find full-time jobs more easily than will those who have no training.

Shoe repairers can advance as they gain experience. Some supervise other workers in a large shoe repair shop. They may also manage the shop. Some experienced workers start their own shoe repair businesses. They can build their businesses by offering more services to customers.

Today, many shoes are made of materials other than leather. Also, some shoes cannot be repaired. For example, the heels on athletic shoes cannot be replaced. These changes have affected the demand for shoe repairers. However, other leather goods are becoming more popular. The need for repairers who can work on orthopedic shoes will increase as well. As a result, the demand for shoe repairers should remain steady. It will be highest for repairers who can perform many different tasks.

For more information on shoe repairers, write to:

Amalgamated Clothing and Textile Workers Union
15 Union Square West
New York, NY 10003
(212) 242–0700

Leather Industries of America
2501 M Street, NW
Washington, DC 20037

Shoe Service Institute of America
1740 East Joppa Road
Baltimore, MD 21234
(301) 661–4400

Chapter 10
Pest Control Worker

Pest control workers inspect buildings for signs of termites, mice, and other pests. If they see signs of these pests, they take action to get rid of them. Many pest control workers are employed by small companies. Some of the companies are branches of nationwide chains. Pest control workers are also employed by large hotels, restaurants, and food-processing plants. Pests are often a problem in buildings where food is stored and cooked. Some government agencies employ pest control workers. These workers inspect and treat government-owned offices and apartment buildings. Pest control workers also help keep homes and other buildings free of pests.

Education, Training, and Salary

Pest control companies prefer to hire people who have a high school education. They look for people who have taken courses in science and business math. These courses can make it easier to learn the job. Pest control workers must have a driver's license and a good driving record.

Pest control workers also benefit from some knowledge of carpentry. The wooden parts of buildings often are attacked by pests. Some workers take carpentry courses in high school. Others may have some construction experience.

69

Most pest control workers train on the job. Some companies begin the training with two or three weeks of classroom instruction. Others require new employees to complete a home-study course. New workers usually work for several months with someone who is more experienced. Then they are able to handle simple jobs alone. However, it may take two or three years of experience to gain a thorough knowledge of pest control. This knowledge is needed to deal with serious pest control problems.

In many states, pest control workers must be licensed. They may need to pass a written test in order to get a license. The test makes sure workers know about proper safety procedures. Most workers who supervise the use of dangerous chemicals must have a license.

Most pest control workers earn between $16,000 and $18,000 a year. Experienced workers can earn $20,000 or more a year. Benefits usually include paid vacations and holidays. Some employers also provide health insurance and a pension plan.

Job Description

Sometimes a building owner may ask a pest control company to make regular inspections for pests. The building may be for sale. Potential buyers usually want to know if pests are a problem. Or the owner of the building may have seen some pests before calling the pest control company.

Pest control workers look for signs of pests. They search attics, basements, and garages as well as the main areas of the building. They may find

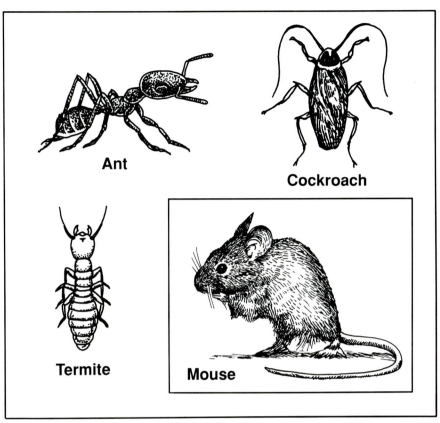

Pest control workers must learn to deal with a variety of insects and animals.

that termites have eaten away some of the wooden structure of the building. Birds may have built nests in vents or other openings. Sometimes ants, rats, mice, or cockroaches are a problem. Pest control workers may even need to deal with wasps or snakes.

If workers find signs of pests, they look further to find where the pests live and how far they have spread. They check to see how much damage the pests have caused. They decide on the best way to get rid of the pests. In most cases, they give the owner of the building an estimate of the cost.

Pest control workers use many methods to get rid of pests. They may use poisonous sprays, powders, or pastes. The workers may have to apply these chemicals under wooden floors or inside walls. If so, they drill holes into the wooden floors or walls. Some pests can be caught in traps. In some places, workers pump chemicals into the ground to keep more pests from entering the building.

Pest control workers must be very careful in their work. Some of the chemicals they use can harm people and pets. Workers must also protect food and water supplies from the chemicals.

Some of the areas that need to be treated are small and dirty. Workers may have to crawl into these places with their equipment. In these situations, workers must take extra care to avoid getting the chemicals they are using on their skin or in their eyes or noses.

It may take several treatments to deal with the problem. Even after the pests are gone, workers may visit the building regularly to make sure the pests have not returned. Often, pest control workers concentrate on the buildings in a certain area. When someone calls, they inspect the building and get rid of the pests.

Outlook for Jobs

Pest control workers can advance as they gain experience. Some supervise the work of less experienced workers. They may manage a branch office of a large pest control company. Some go on to manage a number of branch offices in a region. A few become sales workers for chemical or pest control companies. With more training and some college courses, a worker can specialize in termite control.

People who want to become pest control workers have a bright future. More and more homes, offices, and other buildings are being built. They will need protection from pests. Older buildings need pest control as well. Pest control workers make sure nothing lives in a building except what should be living there.

For more information on pest control workers, write to:

American Entomological Society
1900 Race Street
Philadelphia, PA 19103
(215) 561–3978

American Institute of Biological Sciences
730 Eleventh Street, NW
Washington, DC 20001
(202) 628–1500

National Pest Control Association
8100 Oak Street
Dunn Loring, VA 22024
(703) 573–8330

Chapter 11
Laundry and Dry-Cleaning Worker

Laundry and dry-cleaning workers operate the machines that wash or dry-clean fabric. Most workers do a variety of other tasks as well. Some specialize in one task, such as collecting clothes, ironing shirts, removing spots and stains, or stretching rugs. Others work at the front counter. They accept clothing from customers and return clean clothing to them. They may also act as cashier.

Education, Training, and Salary

Laundry and dry-cleaning workers do not need to meet any educational requirements. Some employers prefer to hire people who have a high school education. Workers who want to advance to supervisor or manager may need a high school education.

Laundry and dry-cleaning workers are trained on the job. In a large company, workers may be trained to do one job. Small companies often train their workers to do several tasks. Some dry-cleaning organizations offer short courses on new cleaning methods.

The starting pay for laundry and dry-cleaning workers averages between $8,500 and $10,000 a year. Experienced dry-cleaning spotters and finishers can earn between $15,000 and $18,000 a year. Large companies may provide paid holidays and vacations. Small companies often do not provide benefits for their employees.

Job Description

All laundry and dry-cleaning workers clean fabric. But the methods they use are different. Laundry workers wash clothes using water and soap. Dry cleaning is used for items that cannot be washed in water. Dry cleaning uses chemicals to clean the clothes. In both methods, the clothes are dried in large dryers.

Laundry and dry-cleaning companies employ workers to do a variety of jobs. Some of these jobs are common to both laundries and dry cleaners.

Route workers pick up clothes, linens, and draperies from customers' homes. They return these items after they have been washed or cleaned. Some route workers collect payment from customers. These workers must have a valid driver's license.

Counter clerks work at the front desk. They take clothes and other items from customers. Some customers give special instructions. The clerks make note of these. For example, a customer may want shirts treated with starch to make them smooth and somewhat stiff. Customers may also say whether shirts should be returned in boxes or on hangers.

Markers place tags on all items brought in for washing or dry cleaning. The tags identify the owner of the item. Markers may also sort the clothing. Some items may need mending. Others have problem stains that must be removed. The markers send the stained items to spotters.

Spotters remove spots and stains from fabric and other materials. They identify the type of fabric and the cause of the stain. Laundry spotters use bleach and detergents to remove the stain. They may use brushes or sponges to apply the cleaning liquids. Dry-cleaning spotters use chemical solutions to remove stains. Then they flush out the chemicals with steam, water, or air pressure. Spotters are more highly trained than other workers are. They must be able to identify fabric and stain types, and they must handle chemicals with care.

Laundry workers take dirty clothes from the markers and spotters. They place them in washing machines, along with the detergent. They may also add bleach and starch to some loads. When a load cycle is complete, the workers operate the extractors that spin most of the water out of the clothes. The next step is the drying cycle. Each of these steps may be done by a different

A counter clerk in a laundry or dry-cleaning shop takes clothes from a customer and may serve as cashier.

Why do some fabrics need to be dry-cleaned? Natural fibers such as linen and silk can absorb water and swell if washed. As they dry, the fibers shrink. A dress that once fit perfectly may be three sizes too small after being washed! Dry-cleaning fluid is not absorbed by these fibers. So the clothes do not swell and shrink.

People dry-clean for another reason. Some stains do not dissolve in water. Lipstick, butter, and other greasy stains must be dry-cleaned. The cleaning fluid can dissolve these oily and fatty stains.

Dry cleaning is not a modern invention. A list of jobs from over 3,000 years ago mentions dry cleaning. A French book from the 1700s tells about a "special secret for removing grease and oil spots from silk stuff."

person. In small laundries, one person may do all these tasks.

Once the clothes are clean, finishers fold and press them. Some finishers work on flat items, such as sheets and tablecloths. Others specialize in more complex items. They use special tools to help press sleeves, collars, and ruffles.

Inspectors make sure the clothes have been cleaned and pressed properly. Then the clothes are placed in protective bags or boxes. The amount owed by each customer is written on a ticket and attached to the clothes.

The dry-cleaning process is much the same. Workers sort the clothes and place them in dry-cleaning machines. They operate valves, levers, and switches to start the machines and send in the cleaning fluid. When the cycle is complete, the items are dried in tumblers, or dryers.

Some dry cleaners also clean rugs. Workers measure each rug before it is cleaned. After the rug is dry, it must be stretched out to its original size.

Outlook for Jobs

Laundry and dry-cleaning workers can learn new skills by taking short courses. These courses are offered by the International Fabricare Institute. They last from a few days to several weeks. As workers gain experience and skill, they may advance to jobs that pay more. Some may become supervisors or managers. A few may be able to open their own businesses.

The demand for laundry and dry-cleaning services will continue to grow. More people are entering the work force. These people have less time to do their own laundry. They also may have more clothes that need to be dry-cleaned. However, new laundry and dry-cleaning equipment requires fewer workers than older machinery does. As a result, the number of jobs will not grow as fast as the need for laundry and dry-cleaning services will.

For more information on laundry and dry-cleaning workers, write to:

Institute of Industrial Launderers
1730 M Street, NW, Suite 610
Washington, DC 20036

International Fabricare Institute
12251 Tech Road
Silver Spring, MD 20904
(301) 622–1900

Chapter 12
Getting the Job: Tips for the Reader

Starting Out

Whatever job you decide to go after, you want to do it to the best of your ability. And you can do this only if you have picked a job you enjoy. Be honest with yourself. Begin your job search by understanding your talents and interests.

Rate Your Strengths

Write down a few lines about yourself. Tell what you like and what you dislike. List your favorite subjects at school and your least favorite subjects. Describe what bores you and what interests you most.

Make a chart and list any jobs you have ever had. Include your supervisors' names, your work addresses, and the dates of employment. Now make a list of your hobbies or interests. Also list the schools you have attended and the activities you take part in. This list would include clubs or teams you have joined. If you have done any volunteer work, be sure to list it. Finally, add to your list the names of any awards or prizes you have won.

List Your Job Possibilities

List all the jobs in this book that sound interesting. Look at each job and see if you qualify. If a job you like requires extra training, write that down. Also check the publications in the back of this book. Write down the titles of any books or other materials that will tell you more about the jobs you like.

Look at your job list and your strengths list. See where they match up. Put a star by those jobs that would use your strengths.

Consult Counselors

Talk to a guidance counselor at your school. Ask about jobs that are open in your field of interest. Your state or local employment service can also help you.

Looking for Work

When you have settled on the jobs you would like, start looking for openings. Apply for as many jobs as you can. The more jobs you apply for, the better your chance of finding one.

Research   Find out everything you can about jobs you are applying for. Learn about the positions, the employers, and the employers' needs. The more you know, the more impressive you will be in your interview.

Ads   There are two types of newspaper classified ads: *help wanted* and *situation wanted.* A help-wanted ad is placed by an employer looking to fill a specific job. It tells you the job title, requirements, salary, company, and whom to contact. You may also see a blind ad, one that

People who place classified ads often use abbreviations. They want to make their ad as short as possible. Read the classified ad section in your newspaper to become familiar with abbreviations. Here is a short list to help you now:

excel. _____ excellent
bnfts. _____ benefits
exp. _____ experience
p.t.
  or p/t _____ part-time
h.s. _____ high school
grad. _____ graduate
w. _____ with
avail. _____ available

f.t.
  or f/t _____ full-time
emp. _____ employment
gd. _____ good
refs. _____ references
ext. _____ extension
req. _____ required
sal. _____ salary
pfd. _____ preferred

does not name the employer. Answer the ad by letter or by phone, as directed in the ad. Follow up within two weeks with another phone call or letter if you have not heard from the employer.

A person looking for work can place a situation wanted ad. This ad tells the kind of work the person is looking for and why he or she qualifies. It also tells when he or she could start working.

Networking   Networking is letting everyone know what jobs you are looking for. Talk to people in your field of interest. Some good leads on jobs can be found this way. Friends and relatives might also be able to help. Follow up on what you learn with a phone call or letter.

Employment Services   Check with your school's placement service for job openings. State and local employment services often have job listings.

Civil Service   Federal, state, and local governments offer many jobs. Find the civil service office near you and ask about openings. See the feature on the top of the next page. It explains more about civil service jobs.

Unions   Find out about labor unions that may be involved with jobs in your field. Check with union locals in your town; you can find phone numbers in the phone book.

Temporary Employment   Working on a temporary basis can lead to other jobs or to part-time or full-time work. Seasonal work is available for many jobs.

84

CIVIL SERVICE

Federal and state governments employ several million workers. In order to get a government job, you must first check with the Federal Job Information Center or a state department of personnel office. Look for an announcement concerning the type of job that interests you. The announcement describes the job. It also lists the education and experience that you will need to qualify for the job.

Once you know about a government job opening, you must fill out an application to take a civil service test. If your application is approved, you must then take and pass the exam. Exams are usually written, but may also be oral. Some exams include essays or performance tests. All exams are tailored to fit a specific job. An exam may cover such items as English usage, reasoning, or clerical or mechanical skills.

Applying in Person

Applying to an employer in person can be a good idea. Call for an appointment. Tell the employer that you would like to have an interview. Some may ask that you send a letter or résumé first.

Sending Letters

Writing letters can also be a good way to ask about jobs. Typed letters are preferred, but neat, handwritten letters are acceptable. Check the Yellow Pages or industry magazines at the public library for addresses. The librarian can help you. Address letters to a company's personnel or human resources department. Send your résumé with the letter. Keep copies of all letters. Follow up in a couple of weeks with another letter.

Résumé

A résumé is a useful one-page outline of information about you. It introduces you to a possible future employer. A résumé should be based on your strengths list. It sums up your education, work history, and skills.

You will enclose your résumé in letters you write to future employers. You also will take it with you to give to your interviewer. Look at the sample résumé on page 87 to see how a typical résumé looks.

Always put your full name, address, and phone number at the top of the résumé. Type the résumé, if possible, or write it by hand neatly. Then state your objective or the job you are applying for. Put down any experience that shows you are a good worker. Volunteer work and part-time jobs tell an employer that you are willing to help out and work hard. Put down your most recent job first.

Finally, include information about your education. You can also list any special skills, awards, or honors you have received.

Writing Letters

When you send your résumé in the mail, always attach a cover letter. Write a short letter, no more than three or four paragraphs. It should come right to the point and lead the employer to your résumé.

Explain what job you are interested in. Include a short listing of your qualifications. Your letter should catch the employer's interest. That way the employer will want to turn to your résumé. See the sample on page 88.

Résumé

Sandra Pelikan
8824 Sloane Avenue
Stuttgart, AL 45678
(205) 555–3498

Objective: To become a master locksmith and home security adviser.

Experience

1990   Worked as store clerk in Stuttgart Hardware and Home Center during summer vacation.

1989–90   Volunteer laborer with community redevelopment project.

Training
Completed a locksmith home-study course. Taking machine shop and design classes at Tri-County Technical School.

Education
1990   Graduated Stuttgart High School.

References available on request.

November 1, 1991
Sandra Pelikan
8824 Sloane Avenue
Stuttgart, AL 45678

Mr. Diego Sanchez
All-Secure Home Systems
80 Main Street
Macon, AL 45768

Dear Mr. Sanchez:

I am answering your advertisement for an apprentice locksmith that appeared in the *Daily Record* on October 30.

I have completed a home-study course in basic lock and key design. My work at Stuttgart Hardware includes cutting keys and selling locks.

My goal is to become a master locksmith. I also want to learn to install and service electronic security systems. I plan to take an evening class in electronics during the fall.

I am enclosing my résumé to give you more information about my background. I look forward to hearing from you at your earliest convenience.

Thank you in advance for your time.

Sincerely,

Sandra Pelikan

enclosure

Completing the Application Form

You may have to fill out an application form when applying for a job. (See the sample on pages 90 and 91.) This form asks for your education, experience, work history, and possibly other information.

The employer may mail an application form to you ahead of time. Or, you may be asked to fill out the form when you come for the interview.

Follow the instructions carefully. Print or type information neatly. Neatness tells the employer that you care about your work. It also shows you can organize information and think clearly.

Have all information with you when you arrive. You will need your Social Security number. You may need to list your past jobs. You will have to give the dates you worked, addresses, and phone numbers.

List your most recent jobs first, as you do on your résumé.

However, do not answer any question that you feel invades your privacy. Laws prevent an employer from asking about certain things. These things include race, religion, national origin, age, and marital status. Questions about your family situation, property, car, or arrest record are also not allowed.

The Interview

The way you act in a job interview will tell the employer a lot about you. It can be the biggest single factor that helps an employer decide whether to hire you. An interview is very impor-

APPLICATION FOR EMPLOYMENT

(Please print or type your answers)

PERSONAL INFORMATION   Date _____

Name _____ Social Security Number _____ / _____ / _____

Address _____
       Street and Number   City   State   Zip Code

Telephone number (_____) _____ – _____ (_____) _____ – _____
                day   evening

Job applied for _____ Salary expected $ _____ per _____

How did you learn of this position? _____

Do you want to work _____ Full time or _____ Part time?

Specify preferred days and hours if you answered part time _____

Have you worked for us before? _____ If yes, when? _____

On what date will you be able to start work? _____

Have you ever been convicted of a crime, excluding misdemeanors and summary offenses?

_____ No _____ Yes

If yes, describe in full _____

Whom should we notify in case of emergency?

Name _____ Relationship _____

Address _____
       Street and number   City   State   Zip Code

Telephone number (_____) _____ – _____ (_____) _____ – _____
                day   evening

EDUCATION

Type of School	Name and Address	Years Attended	Graduated		Course or Major
High School			Yes	No	
College			Yes	No	
Post-graduate			Yes	No	
Business or Trade			Yes	No	
Military or other			Yes	No	

WORK EXPERIENCE (List in order, beginning with most recent job)

Dates		Employer's Name and Address	Rate of Pay Start/Finish	Position Held	Reason for Leaving
From	To				

ACTIVITIES AND HONORS (List any academic, extracurricular, civic, or other achievements you consider significant.)

_____

_____

PERSONAL REFERENCES
_____

Name and Occupation   Address   Phone Number

_____

_____

_____

PLEASE READ THE FOLLOWING STATEMENTS CAREFULLY AND SIGN BELOW:

The information that I have provided on this application is accurate to the best of my knowledge and is subject to validation. I authorize the schools, persons, current employer, and other organizations or employers named in this application to provide any relevant information that may be required to arrive at an employment decision.

_____   _____

Applicant's Signature   Date

tant. Therefore, you should prepare yourself to make a good impression.

Before you go to the interview, prepare what you will say. Think of why you want the job, your experience, and why you qualify. Learn as much about the job and the company as possible. You can do this through ads, brochures, employees, or your library. This will show that you are interested in the company's needs.

Make a list of questions you have. And try to guess what the interviewer will ask. You may ask if you can work overtime or if you can take courses for more training or education. Bring in any certificates or licenses you may need to show.

Dress neatly and appropriately for the interview. Make sure you know exactly where the interview will take place so you will be on time. Allow extra time to get there in case you are delayed by traffic or for some other reason.

Following Up

After the interview, thank the interviewer for his or her time and shake hands. If the job appeals to you, tell the person that you are interested.

When you get back home, send a letter thanking the interviewer for his or her time. Repeat things that were discussed in the interview. Keep a copy of it for yourself and start a file for all future letters.

Think about how you acted in the interview. Did you ask the right questions? Were your answers right? Did you feel you should have done something differently? If so, make notes so you can do better the next time.

If you do not hear from the company in two weeks, write a letter. Tell the interviewer you are still interested in the job. You can also phone to follow up.

Know Your Rights: What Is the Law?

Federal   Under federal law, employers cannot discriminate on the basis of race, religion, sex, national origin, ancestry, or age. People aged forty to seventy are specifically protected against age discrimination. Handicapped workers also are protected. Of course, these laws protect only workers who do their jobs. Employers need not hire workers who are unqualified. And they are free to fire workers who do not perform.

State   Many states have laws against discrimination based on age, handicap, or membership in armed services reserves. Laws differ from state to state. In some states, there can be no enforced retirement age. And some protect people suffering from AIDS.

Applications   When filling out applications, you do not have to answer questions that may invade your privacy. Questions about whether you are married, have children, own property or a car do not have to be answered. Nor do you have to answer questions about an arrest record. An employer may ask, however, if you have ever been convicted of a crime.

At Work   It is against the law for employers to discriminate against workers when setting hours, workplace conditions, salary, hirings, layoffs, firings, or promotions. And no employer can treat a worker unfairly if he or she has filed a discrimination suit or taken other legal action.

Read Your Contract   Read any work contract you are given. Do not sign it until you understand and agree to everything in it. Ask questions if you have them. If you have used an employment agency, find out about fees before you sign a contract. Some agencies will charge you a fee for finding a job. Others charge the employer.

When Discrimination Occurs: What You Can Do

Government Help   Call the Equal Employment Opportunity Commission or the state civil rights commission if you feel you've been discriminated against. If they think you have been unfairly treated, they may take legal action. If you have been unfairly denied a job, you may get it. If you have been unfairly fired, you may get your job back and receive pay that is owed you. Any mention of the actions taken against you may be removed from your work records. To file a lawsuit, you will need a lawyer.

Private Help   Private organizations like the American Civil Liberties Union (ACLU) and the National Association for the Advancement of Colored People (NAACP) fight against discrimination. They can give you advice.

Sources

General Career Information

Abrams, Kathleen S. *Guide to Careers Without College.* New York: Franklin Watts, 1988.

Career Information Center, 4th ed., 13 vols. Mission Hills, Calif.: Glencoe/Macmillan, 1990.

Dubrovin, Vivian. *Guide to Alternative Education and Training.* New York: Franklin Watts, 1988.

Hopke, William E., editor in chief. *The Encyclopedia of Career and Vocational Guidance,* 7th ed., 3 vols. Chicago: Ferguson, 1987.

Littrell, J. J. *From School to Work.* South Holland, Ill.: Goodheart-Willcox, 1984.

Occupational Outlook Handbook. Washington, D.C.: U.S. Government Printing Office, revised biennially.

Perry, Robert L. *Guide to Self-Employment.* New York: Franklin Watts, 1989.

Primm, E. Russell, III, editor in chief. *Career Discovery Encyclopedia,* 6 vols. Chicago: Ferguson, 1990.

Personal Services

Design Occupations. Washington, D.C.: U.S. Government Printing Office, 1982.

Lobb, Charlotte. *Exploring Apprenticeship Careers.* New York: Richard Rosen, 1985.

Sutherland, Douglas. *Professional Catering, Cookery, and Kitchen Practice.* Philadelphia: Trans-Atlantic Publishing, 1987.

Wittenberg, Renee. *Opportunities in Child Care.* Lincolnwood, Ill.: National Textbook Company, 1987.

Index